PAIR-IT BOOKS

Weather

SIGHTS AND SOUNDS

Written by Margaret Fetty

STECK-VAUGHN
ELEMENTARY · SECONDARY · ADULT · LIBRARY
A Harcourt Company

www.steck-vaughn.com

It's a rainy day.
Splish! Splash!

I wear my rain boots.

I walk in water puddles.

It's a sunny day.
Oooh! Aaah!

I wear my tennis shoes.

I play outside.

It's a snowy day.
Scrunch! Crunch!

I wear my mittens.
I build a snowman.

It's a cloudy day.
Huff! Puff!

I wear my jeans.

I look for shapes in the clouds.

It's a cold day.
Brrr! Brrr!

I wear my snowsuit.

I skate on the ice.

It's a breezy day.
Swish! Swoosh!

I wear a turtleneck.
I play in a pile of leaves.

It's a stormy day.
Crash! Boom!

I stay inside where it's safe.

I read a book with my dad.

What's the weather like today?
Look and listen to find out.